A FLAMINGO CHICK GROWS UP

by Joan Hewett
photographs by Richard Hewett

CAROLRHODA BOOKS, INC./MINNEAPOLIS

PUCK HATCHES

Summer is here.

Flamingos crowd around a salty lake.

They build their nests in the mud.

A mother flamingo lays an egg.

The mother sits on the egg.
Then the father sits on the egg.
They protect it from the hot sun.

The flamingo chick hatches
after 30 days.
His name is Puck.
Puck is alert.
His feathers are soft and fluffy.

His mother watches over him.
So does his father.
They take turns.

Puck's father gets up.

He stretches his long legs.

Puck gets up too.

Puck tells his parents he is hungry.

Mother has a kind of milk in her stomach.
It is called crop milk.

She brings the crop milk up into her bill.
She drips it into Puck's mouth.

Snug in his nest,
Puck eats and sleeps.

Puck is 3 days old.

He stands on his big webbed feet.

Is he ready to walk?

He takes a few wobbly steps.

Puck's short legs get stronger.
After 1 week, the chick's steps are steady.

Puck leaves the nest.

He walks down to the salty water.

Long Legs and a Curved Bill

Rosy-pink flamingos stand in the lake.
Chicks wade in the shallow water.

Puck wades in.
He joins the other chicks.

Sometimes, Puck wants to be
with his parents.
He follows them wherever they go.

The chick's legs grow quickly.
Puck is much taller
than he was.
He practices walking
on his long legs.

One afternoon,
a storm blows across the sky.
Thunder rumbles.
Puck is afraid.
He runs back to his mother.

Puck's coat is changing color.
Gray feathers grow in.
They poke up through the white feathers.
Puck's bill is also changing.
It is becoming curved.

Puck combs
his feathers
with his bill.
He cleans
his feathers.

Puck still drinks
crop milk.
He also tries
to eat plants.
Tiny plants float
on the water.
Puck snaps at the
plants with his bill.

Flamingos eat from the lake's muddy bottom.

Tiny plants grow in the mud.

Tiny animals live among the plants.

Flamingos scoop up this stew in their bills.

Puck is 5 weeks old.
His bill is fully formed.
He is ready to scoop up food
from the lake's bottom.

PUCK GROWS NEW FEATHERS

Puck is 7 weeks old.

He spends his days with other chicks.

The chicks eat from the lake.

They rest on the sunbaked shore.

Summer turns to autumn.
Puck is 3 months old.
His coat is changing.
Longer gray feathers are coming in.
The feathers have a hint of pink.

A flamingo's flying feathers
are long and black.
When Puck spreads his wings,
they are easy to see.

It is winter.

Puck has his first pink and black coat.

The flamingo chick is growing up.

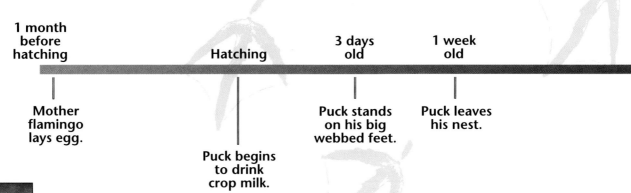

| 1 month before hatching | Hatching | 3 days old | 1 week old |

Mother flamingo lays egg.

Puck begins to drink crop milk.

Puck stands on his big webbed feet.

Puck leaves his nest.

More about Flamingos

Flamingos have very long legs. They are wading birds. They wade though shallow water. They feed on tiny plants and animals that live on the bottom of salty lakes.

Flamingos have long necks. Their necks bend and flex like a rubber hose. Flamingos also have big bills. Their bills curve down. When flamingos feed, they hold their heads upside down and scoop up food in their bills.

Flamingos like hot weather. They are tropical birds. Wild flamingos live together in huge flocks. In east Africa, thousands and thousands of flamingos have lived and raised their chicks on the muddy shores of Nakuru Lake.

Flamingos are easily spooked. Bossy storks may drive flamingos from their nesting grounds. A low-flying airplane may frighten them. Even so, scientists believe there are still millions of wild flamingos. The birds live in remote, faraway places. So few people ever see them.

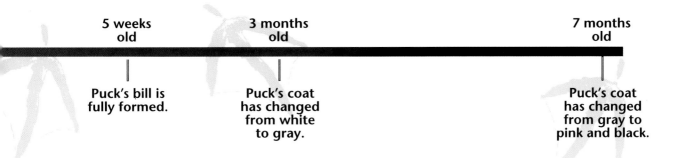

5 weeks old	3 months old	7 months old
Puck's bill is fully formed.	Puck's coat has changed from white to gray.	Puck's coat has changed from gray to pink and black.

Puck is a Caribbean flamingo. Caribbean flamingos live on islands in the Caribbean and on the coast of northeastern South America. Adult Caribbean flamingos are the most brightly colored flamingos. They have beautiful orange-pink and reddish feathers.

Flocks of wild Caribbean flamingos once lived in Florida. But the birds were hunted for their brilliant feathers. All of the wild Caribbean flamingos in Florida were killed.

More about Wild Animal Parks

Puck lives in a wild animal park called Busch Gardens. The park is in Tampa, Florida. It is home to more than 300 Caribbean flamingos. When the flamingo chicks are a few days old, their wing feathers are clipped. This keeps the flamingos from flying away.

At Busch Gardens, flamingos build mud nests and lay eggs. They sit on and hatch their eggs. They feed and take care of their chicks. Even though they don't fly, the birds behave much as they would in the wild.

To Orson Ridgely Hewett, our first grandchild

This book is available in two editions:
Library binding by Carolrhoda Books, Inc.,
  a division of Lerner Publishing Group
Soft cover by First Avenue Editions,
  an imprint of Lerner Publishing Group
241 First Avenue North
Minneapolis, MN 55401 U.S.A.

Website address: www.lernerbooks.com

Library of Congress Cataloging-in-Publication Data

Hewett, Joan.
  A flamingo chick grows up / by Joan Hewett ; photographs by Richard Hewett.
     p.   cm.
   ISBN 1-57505-164-8 (lib. bdg. : alk. paper)
   ISBN 0-8225-0090-6 (pbk. : alk. paper)
   1. Flamingo—Infancy—Juvenile literature. [1. Flamingos. 2. Animals—Infancy.] I. Hewett, Richard, ill. II. Title.
   QL696.C56 H49 2002
   598.3'5—dc21   00-011445

Manufactured in the United States of America
1 2 3 4 5 6 – JR – 07 06 05 04 03 02